HOW TO BECOME MASTER OF SPEECHES & TALKS

THE SUBTLE ART OF PUBLIC SPEAKING

HOW TO BECOME
MASTER OF SPEECHES & TALKS

THE SUBTLE ART OF PUBLIC SPEAKING

AUTHORED BY
AUTHOR SHERRY

Penman Books

Office No. 303, Kumar House Building,
D Block, Central Market, Opp PVR Cinema,
Prashant Vihar, Delhi 110085, India
Website: www.penmanbooks.com
Email: publish@penmanbooks.com

First Published by Penman Books 2020
Copyright © Author Sherry 2020
All Rights Reserved.

Title: How to Become Master of Speeches & Talks
ISBN: 978-93-89024-71-5

DEDICATION

Nobody writes a book entirely alone without support.

I dedicate this book to all my family members, followers, mentors and mentees and all the public speakers around the globe for their support and trust in me.

It takes a lot of effort to publish a book with acute research, practical knowledge and skills shared. I am thankful to God for navigating me to the platform of public speaking and making my dream of writing a book on public speaking come true.

My special thanks to my publisher – Penman Books for helping me to bring this book out in the market.

I am grateful to all of you, including you, the reader. Without you, this book wouldn't have been transported to the shelf. Please enjoy reading. Live with pride and prosper!

To your success,

Author Sherry

CONTENTS

SECTION TWO: PRACTICE

SECTION THREE: PRESENT

PRAISES FOR THE BOOK

"Author Sherry has a great hold on communication and his coaching is par excellence. If it is Public speaking, it is only Author Sherry."

—Kiran Chopra,
Director and Chairperson -Punjab Kesari

~ ~ ~

"The book offers what any aspiring speaker could need, masterful and multifaceted elucidation of speeches and talks; in short, Public Speaking. Author Sherry has brilliantly summarized the elements of speaking, from speech preparation to fears a speaker may come across while being on stage, and much more. If you want to become a fine speaker, this book surely is a doorway to all that you should be knowing. Kudos Author Sherry!"

—Him-eesh Madan,
Motivational Speaker, Entrepreneur

~ ~ ~

"An inspiration for youth and an iconic coach of public speaking and communication. His interaction at our college has changed student's perspectives."

—Dr. PS Chauhan,
Director – IPS College, Gwalior

"Author Sherry is a master storyteller and an excellent public speaking coach. Never come across better than him."

—Piyush Sachdeva, *Director, Josh Talks*

~ ~ ~

"Author Sherry walks the talk as a coach and this book is a proof of it. His interactions with me are precious. I finally found someone so passionate about public speaking. I call Author Sherry - 'Badshah of public speaking.' I shared the stage with him at TEDx and witnessed thunderous applause after his talk as a speaker. He was mind-blowing."

—Major Mohommed Ali Shah,
Bollywood Actor, Highest TEDx Talks Speaker, MS Talks Speaker, Josh Talks Speaker

~ ~ ~

"If you want to be a great public speaker, you need an authentic mentor and I found him. What a book! What a man! Go for Author Sherry."

—Jas Brar, *International Speaker, Blogger, Educator - London*

~ ~ ~

"Author sherry for me means - Motivation to thousands of people to move ahead in their life and his Book is always amazing for people who wish to learn excellent public speaking and feel like changing their life by upgrading their skills. As I am Being Hair-stylist, I always follow his tips for public speaking as my mentor which has supported me for my business enhancement as well."

—Neel David Katwal,
International Hairstylist, MS Talks Speaker, Director – Neel David Group, Nepal

~ ~ ~

"Excellent content with some amazing tips on public speaking. Author Sherry's work is outstanding. - If you really want to become a public speaker, you shouldn't waste a single minute.. read this book and meet Author Sherry. He is the man to learn from."

—Jolly Uncle,
Motivational writer, Graphologist

~ ~ ~

"Strong Content and really appealing presentation with very effective techniques shared.No.1 skill in the world today is public speaking and being a public speaking coach Author Sherry has done splendid work."

—Gulraj Singh Shahpuri,
Business Coach, Trainer, Author, Entrepreneur

~ ~ ~

"Simply awesome, a must-read for anyone who interacts with people. Author Sherry is changing lives through public speaking coaching and his brand MS Talks."

—Rajeev Narang,
CEO -AIPL Brandbuzz, TEDx Speaker,
MS Talks Speaker

~ ~ ~

"15 amazing chapters of this book can change the way you speak in public. Author Sherry conveyed his thoughts on the subject in most simple words, but yet in an amazing, appealing & eloquent way. After going through the chapters I found myself in my younger days speaking anywhere & everywhere possible again and again encouraging me bit by bit. What more could I say!! God bless you!"

—Advocate Subhash Sharma,
Social Activist, Josh Talks Speaker,
Secretary General – MS Talks India

~ ~ ~

"'Speech' is a creative art, and 'Talk' is a subtle art. Put it together mildly - 'A creatively subtle art'. One can master it. Go for the Book and the Mentor."

—Mukesh Bhatnagar,
Writer and Storyteller, Secretary- MS Talks India

~ ~ ~

"Author Sherry is transforming lives through his writing and coaching of public speaking. He is an exceptionally creative person, understands the pain area of people so well. A thorough professional and a genius in his field."

—Prachi Singh,
Image Consultant, MS Talks Speaker

~ ~ ~

"Public speaking is his forte. Author Sherry has mastered it. Go for the book."

—Vandana Narang,
International Trainer and Coach,
MS Talks Speaker

WHAT MENTEES HAVE TO SAY?

"I cannot express enough gratitude for having a mentor like Author Sherry."
I've been learning from Author Sherry since a few months now and I have seen a magical change in my confidence and personality. I've achieved heights I could never imagine of and I'm a proud public speaker now. Not just public speaking, he has been a support in every new risk I've tried to attempt. There's one thing for sure, I'm heading towards the brighter side of my life under his supervision. I cannot express enough gratitude for having a mentor like Author Sherry.

—Shruti Verma, *New Delhi,*
Corporate executive in an IT firm,
Public speaker & Artist.

~ ~ ~

"Outstanding public speaking coach –
Highly recommend his work for everyone."
Author Sherry is a public speaking coach who gives personal attention to his mentees. He guides you on various aspects like body language, non-verbal clues, tone, pitch, intonation etc. He takes you from where you are to where you ought to be.

—Major(Retd) Pradeep Khare,
Ghaziabad, Army Veteran, Blogger,
Columnist, Author and You Tuber.

~ ~ ~

*"From a small-town boy to a public speaker and trainer. The
man behind my success is Author Sherry Sir."*
*When I joined him for public speaking coaching and improving
my communication skills, I was nervous about public speaking
and had stage fright but after a few classes, my confidence was
high. Now I have delivered a keynote speech at the International
Public Speaking Championship 2019 event successfully. I would
like to thank you for your extra ordinary training methods
which helped me to become a Keynote Speaker.*

—Devendra Kumar, Gurugram,
*Keynote Speaker, Software Developer in
Fortune 500 IT company.*

~ ~ ~

*"A great mentor – I am blessed to be a mentee
of such a multitasker!!"*
*Public Speaking is like a sport. You only get better
with practice. Author Sherry sir makes it so easygoing
with his simple and fun-loving techniques. His effective ways as
a mentor make me an enthusiast to learn
more about this subject. Blessed to be a mentee of
such a multitasker!!*

—Swarleen Kaur, *Dehradun,*
Educator, Content Writer, Public Speaker

~ ~ ~

*"I became a motivational speaker, just because
Author Sherry sir is my mentor."
Author Sherry sir is an excellent coach. He is friendly
and at the same time very professional at his work. I came to
him for improving my skills in public speaking and
he has changed me and helped me to speak in front of more than
100 people. I am confident in giving
speeches now as a motivational speaker.*

*—**Santosh Kumar,** Bahadurgarh,
HR Professional, Advocate and Direct Sales Leader*

PREFACE

"The foremost skill which has the power to change your attitude and altitude in success is public speaking."

—Author Sherry

If you have been struggling to understand how can you become a public speaker, motivational speaker or professional speaker you have picked the right book for yourself.

If you have been confused, unplanned, lacking direction or thinking public speaking is tough for you, then I must tell you that after reading this book you will find all the solutions to your problems.

I really don't know which country you belong to, but all I know is I care for you. You may be working into your business, serving as a corporate executive, a known freelancer, a working professional or still pursuing studies in a college or university, but in any case, you are ready for a change.

HOW DO I COME TO KNOW?

Because you are reading this book to change your thought process and you are eager to learn about public speaking. You have signaled that you are ready for help.

Public speaking is the most important skill in the world today.

I assure you that my words written in this book will inspire you to take action and that's all what matters in any area of life to improve. If you trust me which I know you do and as you are going to read this book, you will definitely appreciate the simple language used no matter which country you belong to.

I have already written and published 2 books, both available on *www.amazon.com* .

Unleash the hidden potential – A self-help book on personal development and life skills.

Public Speaking Basics –Talking about the basic aspects of public speaking.

This is my 3rd book in your hand or in front of your eye in case it's an e-book you picked up.

WHAT'S INSIDE THIS BOOK?

I have divided this book into 3 parts and this will give you clarity on how to go through the book. I call it as 3P's of public speaking.

PREPARE - PRACTICE - PRESENT

Prepare to get rid of temporary fear.

(Knowing what to do)

Practice to sound like an expert.

(Journey to become an expert in public speaking)

Present like a king and win your audience.

(Rock the stage)

My name is Author Sherry. I work as one of the authority and a lifetime student of public speaking in India and through this book, I intend to help you to learn the prime art of public speaking. You will break free those negative notions in your head how will I speak, what will I speak, how long I can speak and with whom I will speak.

This book is going to be your one-stop solution to everything you need to become an authority in the public speaking arena.

It took me more than 2 years to create this book, the reason is - I learned practically, implemented everything beforehand and I am eligible to advise you to start your journey of speaking.

I have invested my time reading, doing and simultaneously attending workshops, seminars both as an organizer and a professional speaker.

A simple formula I followed - Learning, doing, teaching at the same time.

I feel proud when I call myself as a professional speaker as I am into full time speaking business now. It is a skill and anyone who is obsessed can learn the art of public speaking just like a skill of learning a sport, playing an instrument, becoming an actor.

It has been a little over 7 years with my total professional speaking experience since the time I became a trainer, but let me tell you that mentoring and training was always my passion during my corporate tenure with my team.

In pursuit of my journey of public speaking, I realized that professional public speaking, personal coaching and mentoring was my call and God has answered it by giving me the opportunity to serve all my countrymen and people abroad.

I believe to invest in my Sundays, deciding not to sit at home and watch television, waste my time thinking about dreams and not working on it.

I compromised with my comforts in order to learn more because I knew what I was doing and becoming. I have never doubted myself.

HOW I RELAX AND REINFORCE POSITIVITY?

It's a busy life and mind needs a quick boost or recharge regularly.

There is a place near my home and I sit there often for my meditation, self-talk exercises, visualizing my success and feeling the nature, smelling flowers sitting in the shadow of trees, walking on sand without footwear and paying gratitude for what I have in my life. I believe emotional intelligence is extremely important for every individual to learn and in public speaking, it is a must skill to have in your arsenal.

I have keen interest in reading more about psychology, meta-physics, sub-conscious mind, human behavior, helping others and spreading happiness and positivity. I am active on social media and create healthy discussions through my posts. I love my family a lot.

FAMILY OF 3 GENERATION OF AUTHORS

It's a rare feat in the sense, God has bestowed his kindness to give the sense of writing to my family. I am thankful to God that I belong to a family of 3 generations of authors. My father, myself and my daughter at the age of 8 has written her maiden book. My mother's contribution might be unnoticed here, but I must tell you she has been the biggest inspiration of my life and she inspired all three of us in many ways to write.

HELPING NEW AUTHORS

My observation is; reading is losing ground to videos. People are gradually getting more involved in watching videos and television.

My message to all of you and especially the young generation is; please keep your reading habits intact and reading minimum 2 books a month. Reading will help you build strong connections, communicate better and create and master intelligent conversations.

From the last 14 months, I am following a principle to buy a book of any new author every month to contribute to the success of book sales for authors and off-course learning from them.

PROFESSIONAL CAREER

Frankly, I never thought I will become an author in my life but it all happened when I decided to move on from the banking sector to corporate training. I have served various departments in corporates and worked with banking, telecom, e-commerce, education, insurance sectors.

I have spoken on top platforms, fortune 500 companies, business schools, universities, colleges. I feel fortunate to say that I had been consistent while attending more than 250 different workshops, training sessions offline and online to gain insights of market trends, sharpen my speaking abilities, communication in last 5 years which I claim is a kind of attainment apart from reading habits of blogs and quality books.

My highest crowd engaged with till now is speaking in front of 500+ people in an auditorium where I presented the Importance of Social Media Marketing and personal branding. I know it is not much by high standards but I am ecstatic and proud of myself that a boy who could barely speak in front of the public has done it.

Since 2017, I organize public speaking conferences and I run my startup with veteran core team members at 'MS Talks India'(MST). The tagline for MST is - Inspiration from anywhere.

Through MST, I have the vision to create an ecosystem to remove stage fright, promote presentation literacy, public speaking, learning new skills which are in demand for personal growth and sharing real stories of people through storytelling.

MY MISSION

By heart, I am a true patriot and want to see every Indian becoming an effective communicator. I want to do everything living in my country and avoid diaspora.

There is huge potential in our country to do any business and that is the reason you see foreign players are collaborating multiple businesses in India. I see a huge potential for coaching and training industry which I feel is scattered at the moment.

Communication and public speaking should be our core strength and as Indians so that we can speak in front of people from abroad freely without any challenge and doubts. I know it's not easy as it sounds but then your mission has to be beyond your imagination and I want that to happen for India.

We deserve. India deserves.

I am all set and working on bringing a movement in India.

My mission is; "To create 1 million speakers in India by 2030."

Broadly, I work in the area of personal growth and human development and public speaking is my passion now. Professional speaking is the next big industry in India. Professional speaking means any individual who is into full time speaking and earn through it.

I have a firm belief that as a reader if you are not reading something which inspires you to measure oneself and transform it is actually not even worth a read. Don't worry, if you just read this book, you will have clarity and success is all about clarity of thoughts.

WHY PUBLIC SPEAKING?

Is it because I have written the book and I am a professional speaker now. No, No, No that is not true my friend. How can I be so mean?

The truth is Public speaking is a must-have skill to adapt and communicate effectively. Please note I said it's a 'skill.'

Notice the top executives and entrepreneurs around you. Most of the successful leaders are great public speakers. Prime Minister Sh. Narendra Modi from India is a great example and goes to show how important public speaking is for each one of us.

Any information given in this book is my personal experience and I have used metaphors mostly where I have been there personally and observed people doing public speaking.

Anywhere if you don't agree to a point, you may simply discard the information.

I believe am still learning and it will always be a part of my life.

This is also one of the key learning from this book that never claims yourself to be an expert. It blocks your learning and you wouldn't even come to know at a sub-conscious level. Remain humble and you will never stumble.

So, are you ready and excited to become a master of talks and speeches?

Thanks for your YES!! Let's begin.

THE INCIDENT THAT CHANGED MY LIFE

13 years back, when I was working for the ICICI group in India, I achieved some sales targets and was selected amongst the top 200 managers in the country.

My girlfriend that time was also part of the function who came with me in my car.

One of my friends was also a part of it and the entire room was full of high energy and happiness to get felicitation from the country-head himself.

When my name was announced, I started walking towards the podium and was feeling so confident and happy that my name has been announced with thunderous clapping everywhere.

I didn't imagine that this moment will become a turning-point in my public speaking career.

When the country-manager shared about my achieved targets and invited me on the podium to share a few words about;

How I achieved the feat and became one of the top 3 managers in Delhi?

What strategy did I follow?

What was running through my mind during the journey of my accomplishment?

I had everything in my mind but the moment I walked on the podium, I received the award.

I was on cloud 9!!

I wanted to share with people about my journey.

I told myself, this was the moment I was looking for.
But after a few seconds,

I started feeling the anxiety to speak and share my journey.

Butterflies started flying in my stomach.

I started feeling shivering in my legs with sweaty hands.

I was unsure what was happening but somehow I survived by escaping with a mild smile, uttering that I don't have anything to share at the moment and indicated my apprehension to speak.

Obviously, my girlfriend was the part of the crowd and wanted me to speak a few words but I couldn't.

I never shared this story with anyone ever as I was shy to talk about my weaknesses, not realizing it actually got me moving in my life.

That day, I realized that someday in my life I am going to share my speeches with the world.

When I left from there, I sat in my car. My girl-friend held my hands with a supportive smile. I said to my girl-friend in a staid tone,

"This will never happen to me again. I have to learn how to speak in public."

Today, I have not only overcome public speaking fear but have also spoken at various prestigious platforms.

I have created a coaching system and following my passion for coaching, mentoring on public speaking and helping people around become effective speakers.

I have also created a platform for speakers to share their real-life stories -MS Talks. I have also coached TEDx speakers in India for their speeches and preparations.

My readers,

I wish the success for you and that is why I have written this book to make sure I am not leaving my learning up to my individual success. I want to spread what I have learned to make you understand how actually public speaking works and it is a skill that anyone can learn and apply as I have.

ABOUT THE AUTHOR

*"I am no public speaking expert.
I am an expert public speaking student."*

—*Author Sherry*

Author Sherry is working as a renowned Public Speaking Coach and TEDx Speakers Coach in India. Through his transformational coaching style, he has provided a speaking platform to many aspiring speakers and created many public speakers in India till now. His clients are working with fortune 500 companies, running successful businesses and professionals in various fields.

Author Sherry works in the area of personal growth and human development and working on a mission to create one million public speakers in India by 2030

Author Sherry is 3 times national award winner and International award-winning coach.

- Featured on BRAG magazine in USA, as an International Influencer of the year 2020.

- Progressive Sikh of the year award by YPSF in association with PTC Punjab.

- Acharya Chanakya Award declared Best Public Speaking Coach in the Country

- Achievers Award for Best Public Speaking Coach in the country by Sh. Manoj Tiwari

Featured on 200+ prestigious platforms of India for his keynote and professional speaking sessions in last 5 years of his successful career and delivered more than 400 workshops, offline, online training sessions in a span of last 8 years of his speaking and training career and trained more than 20,000 professionals across the globe.

- 3 times International TEDx Speaker till 31st January, 2020
- 3 times Josh Talks Speaker
- Belongs to a family of 3 generations of authors
- 170k+ global followers on social media handles
- Professional Speaker, Corporate Facilitator, Author, Certified Communication Coach, Certified NLP Practitioner, Certified Life Coach.

Lead Trainer, CEO: *MS Talks Training & Consulting*

Founder, President & Organizer: *MS Talks India*

- Curator of 5 signature programs on public speaking in India.
- International Public Speaking Championship
- International Kids Talent hunt – public speaking
- MS Talks – Inspirational Talks
- MS Talks – I-inspire annual conference and awards
- Stage Craft – Public Speaking Mastery

I am also serving as an Industry Mentor for Public Speaking, Communication Skills & Employability Skills for premier institutions of India like;

- UPES - Dehradun
- Chandigarh Group of Colleges - Punjab

- New Delhi Institute of Management - Delhi
- Lovely Professional University- Punjab
- Institute of Professional Studies - Gwalior.
- ITS – Ghaziabad
- RKGIT - Ghaziabad

I hope you will enjoy reading my book and if you wish to appoint me for public speaking coaching or mentoring;

Or for any individual session at your company being a sought-after speaker, trainer, facilitator;

Or want MS Talks to organize a session in your corporation with a bunch of specialized speakers;

Feel free to speak to me directly on 9811099884 or write to me at ceo@authorsherry.com, or my team member at mstalksindia@gmail.com.

I have my office in New Delhi, India and would love to serve you.

www.authorsherry.com

www.mstalkstraining.com

www.mstalksindia.com

FOREWORD

Are you ready to seize opportunities to speak? In 2017, right after I was awarded the title of World Champion of Public Speaking in Vancouver, after competing against 35,000 speakers from 142 countries two things happened instantly, which is a reminder for all speakers including me. Firstly, as soon as I collected my award, I was asked to deliver an acceptance speech instantly in front of 2,000 people in the audience, and 10,000 people watching live around the world. I delivered my acceptance speech in which I thanked my mentors, and numerous people who played a part in my success. Many people told me that acceptance speech was the best acceptance speech they have ever heard. Little did they know that I had come prepared to deliver the acceptance speech – it was revised and rehearsed for a few times! Then something else happened, unexpectedly – and it was a world of difference. As soon I was ushered out of the ballroom, a TV crew ambushed me and thrust a microphone in front of my face to conduct an impromptu interview – on camera! I was not expecting that – and was not well prepared for that moment. What do you when you are not prepared to speak? Do you fail to seize opportunities to speak? Do you run out of words to say? Do you run away, and hide?

Fortunately, with the right mindset, and techniques you can speak, even without preparation. Public speaking is a skill anyone can learn. But, only a few will ever take action! Having decided to take the first step to master this skill, you are certainly one among the few who are taking action.

When Sherry reached out to me to write this foreword, I was eager to support him because his mission to help others become speakers resonates well with what I do myself. In this book, Sherry has well documented his journey from being someone who was at the loss of words on stage, embarrassing even his lady love, to someone who can confidently speak in front of a large audience. The best part is that he is willing to share what he learned and reveal the source of his wisdom for the benefit of his readers. That's the true mark of a speaker and author – to share your learning for the benefit of others. This book has something to offer for both the beginner and the master. Read the book, master the techniques, empower yourself, and others. The world needs to hear your views.

As you start your speaking journey, you might wonder "Will this work for me?" As I say in The Mousetrap Way, *You are never too small to be BIG.* If you want to become a better speaker, you better speak. Seek out the best mentor you can find. Ask for help! Be open to feedback and never stop learning. As Sherry says *"Be an Expert Public Speaking Student"*. Let Sherry's book get you started on your journey to the stage.

I am looking forward to seeing you on the big stage and meeting you in person soon!

—Manoj Vasudevan

Next Level Leadership Readiness Expert,
World Champion of Public Speaking,
CEO Thought Expressions, Author of International Bestsellers,
How To Become The World Champion of Public Speaking &
Mastering Leadership The Mousetrap Way

SECTION ONE
PREPARE

CHAPTER ONE

PUBLIC SPEAKERS ARE EVERYWHERE

*"Wherever I find public and observe any speaking going on,
I turn on my student mode."*

—Author Sherry

Public speaking can be a supreme self-esteem booster and a way to transform lives around.

Public speaking engagements are great places to meet elite, new social and professional contacts to transact for the future.

If you would like to change the world, remember - public speaking is an effective platform for spreading revolutionary ideas and inspiring the world.

Public Speaking lets you earn more money than you can ever think of in your life.

You are surrounded by many public speakers around you. You met many in your journey and will meet a lot of them ahead. They have superior qualities which can be used in public speaking.

When I noticed and analyzed what I am going to share with you just now, even I was also surprised. These people exist around us only.

Public speaking happens in small and large groups, apart from seminars, workshops with hundreds and thousands of people. Many great speakers improved through group speaking first and then went on becoming specialists in their niche of speaking.

INTRODUCING SOME COMMON PROFILES OF PUBLIC SPEAKERS AROUND US

1. Scripture reader in Sikh Temple: I have grown up attending a public reading of scriptures at Sikh temples. The readers pick one or two lines to speak and narrate the Sikh religion history very well. Some readers *(paathis)* are so influencing and gifted. I have seen strong feelings of acceptance in God by attendees, people do cry, bow their heads in front of almighty *(Guru)* when they connect to the narrator's point.

Learning for a public speaker: Take one or two main headlines which are enough to do public speaking for 20-60 minutes in front of a larger audience.

2. Anchor: Many anchors are great speakers. The best thing I have observed about them is they enjoy what they do. This attitude sets them free within their mind and succor to communicate authentically. Their energy is contagious. Mr. Manish Paul is a nice example with such a gifted ability to entertain and connect with the audience.

Learning for a public speaker: If you wish to connect with others on the common ground know and like yourself.

3. Radio jockey (RJ): RJ's spread fun through voice on radio stations by helping to reduce the stress of listeners by the way they use their throats. They love speedy and meaningful talk. One of my friends Ms. Devika Dutta from All India Radio – Akashvani is an influential Radio Jockey.

Learning for a public speaker: Learn to use 'Voice modulation' for your success in public speaking.

4. News presenter: Mr. Arnab Goswami, Journalist –Republic TV, is splendid when it comes to persuading though group speaking with dignitaries and celebrities in the newsroom.

Learning for a public speaker: Listening is as important as speaking for public speaking success.

5. Spiritual Teacher: A few years ago, I visited a place Anand Dham Ashram (religious exertion) in New Delhi, India and met a Hindu spiritual teacher – *Shri Sudhanshu Ji Maharaj.* While attending his session, I found out that he is a great **storyteller.** He has a good understanding of Ayurveda products and he spoke about how people got relieved from health problems by using Ayurveda medicines of his brand. Post-session, many people end up buying products of his owned brand –'Yugrishi'. Many other spiritual teachers who do public speaking at large leverage it for other bonafide purposes. Shri Gaur Gopal Das is another good example of an effective public speaker with a similar background serving as a monk.

Learning for a public speaker: You can leverage your message and accelerate business sales through persuasive speaking for public speaking success.

6. Coaching faculty: 15 years back, I was preparing for the Railway examination to crack a government job. I have fond memories of a local student coach in Subhash Nagar, New Delhi. He used to teach 200 students in a hall at one time. The simple formula he used in teaching and speaking:

- Explaining tough logics using familiar examples that are easy to grasp.
- Making students laugh and smile in between to keep the atmosphere lighter.
- Making average and below-average students feel comfortable through engagement.

The result – Many averages and below-average students cleared the examination and got government jobs with decent salaries and used to come to meet him with gifts, sweet boxes to take his blessings.

Learning for a public speaker: Use 10th-grade student language (easy language) to convey your message for public speaking success.

7. Sales leaders: Since I have a sales job background, I have learned a lot from other sales leaders whom I have worked with. They know exactly how to convert a *'no' to a 'yes'*; using supreme speaking skills. They are inquisitive to earn and get fame. Senior leaders in the corporate I have worked with, I found them to be wonderful public speakers especially when they are addressing larger teams in town hall meetings and award nights.

Learning for a speaker: Confidence is a key source for your professional success and public speaking gives you extreme confidence in your career especially in leadership roles

8. Influencers: Jay Shetty, an Indian British guy, a former monk and a motivational speaker from the UK is the no.1 choice of today's generation. Shetty has become one of the world's most popular influencers. In 2017, he was named in the *Forbes* magazine 30-under-30 for being a game-changer in the world of media. In 2018, he had the #1 video on Facebook with over 360 million views. His social media following totals over 32 million, he has produced over 400 viral videos which have amassed more than 5 billion views, and his podcast, *On Purpose*, is consistently ranked the world's #1 Health and Wellness podcast. You will find many spiritual masters as outstanding storytellers who have learned how to influence the audience quick off the mark.

Learning for a speaker*: Use videos for public speaking influence as it is one of the key tools for public speaking success.*

CHAPTER TWO

PRINCIPLES OF PUBLIC SPEAKING

"Communication sometimes is not what you first hear, listen not just to the words, but listen for the reason."

—Catherine Pulsifer

COMMUNICATION MODEL IN PUBLIC SPEAKING

The simplest way to excel in public speaking is to transform your communication style and thoughts. For engaging the audience or effective delivery for a standing ovation by the audience, you need to fine-tune your communication - both verbal and non-verbal skills.

Listening is hearing with attention which is often ignored. However, in public speaking listening can make you a superstar if you listen with attention and respond with accuracy.

To get a better understanding of communication, professor of psychology **Albert Mehrabian** studied the importance of non-verbal communication in the 1970s.

Experts confess that the outcome of this study is the fundamental of the communication model whenever we are standing in front of people to do public speaking.

It has three components that decide the effectiveness of communication, whenever we are speaking from the stage.

1. The content
2. Body language
3. Vocal variety

But in this study, Albert Mehrabian has given the percentage of each component as per their contribution toward effective communication. Many times I ask people to guess the percentages and it is confusing because majorly everyone ends up giving a maximum percentage to the content.

As per **Communication Model study of Albert,**

The content is only 7%, body language is 55% and vocal is 38%. So it means 93% of what decides the effectiveness of communication, we don't practice.

This certainly doesn't mean that content is not important. Content is definitely important and in fact, content is the king in your talk.

But what it means is that even if you have the world's best content or world's best PowerPoint presentation or world's best story and if your body language, expressions, gestures, and vocal variety are not synchronized with the content you might not be able to communicate effectively in front of your audience.

In an interview, Ace investor Warren Buffett gave a piece of advice for young graduates and no it is not about stock investment or portfolio building.

It's an interpersonal skill — communication.

Warren said, "Improving one's communication skills is the easiest way for youngsters just starting out on their professional paths to increase their worth by 50 percent."

PRINCIPLES OF PUBLIC SPEAKING

"You can speak well if your tongue can deliver the message of your heart."

—John Ford

Imagine you are in front of the audience, and if you fumble with the remote of your laptop, get confused by your own slides, or apologize for not being more prepared for the presentation, you are making it clear that you are not worthy of their attention.

Do you think your job is to provide information when you deliver a speech or presentation? Too many speakers make this common mistake. Rather than focusing on the content, your task consists of something else entirely: it is to influence your audience and that is very much achievable by following simple techniques to gain attention.

You can influence when you know about their profile and mindset or in other words either you use certain words familiar with their experience or relatively make it simple so that anyone in the audience can understand your point.

That may mean informing, prompting, directing, envisioning, inspiring, reassuring them or any of dozens of other purposes.

But it's always the human connection that matters.

My desire is first to help you learn the principles behind connecting with others in public speaking;

Empathy: Empathy has Latin and Greek roots. Em, that is derived from the Latin, means – "to see through", and pathy has been derived from the Greek, which means "the eye of the other".

So to empathize here means to understand your audience and see through their eyes.

Expanding your connecting vocabulary beyond just words: Choosing the right words, with the right people, at the right time in the right manner.

Energy never lies: Feel the vibe, the audience indicates you in between what they want you to speak. Work on the room energy to build a connection with people.

Use the right tone: Energy itself is a powerful tool. Some speakers feel loudness means energy. Don't misunderstand loudness with energy. Gain insights into how great connectors connect in your field.

Smile: Van Edwards a behavioral investigator with the science of people, found that speakers who smiled more were rated as more intelligent. It is contagious.

You may follow professional public speakers like; Eric Edmeades, Matt Abrahams Lisa Nichols, Les Brown, John Maxwell, Bob proctor. Check how they connect for public speaking. I am a big fan of Late Jim Rohn, dean of personal development – seen all his tapes, audios and read all his books. Jim is a mentor to me and I follow his teachings. I like reading stuff from John Maxwell, Carmine Gallo and other great communication experts.

Now, I'll help you acquire the practical skills of connection:

- Finding common ground
- Use brevity wherever possible
- Keep the audience surprised wherever possible.
- Make your communication simple
- Capture people's interest

- Inspire the audience
- Remain authentic

These are things anyone can learn to do.

SCRIPTED OR SPONTANEITY?

The top quality of the best speakers is they sound spontaneous. But are they originally spontaneous or they rehearsed brilliantly?

Ahhh… Secret! :)

Nay! It is not a secret anymore, because I am revealing it you right here.

Our brains run much faster and generate thoughts at a lightning speed. I have experienced myself and spoken to various sought after speakers who confess that we forget what we rehearse many times, that is the reason we jump over to a different point which is not rehearsed and sometimes doesn't connect to the topic or say the things stored in our subconscious.

This is why it is said, read your subject thoroughly; you never know which point comes out of your mouth automatically without asking you and it becomes a memory for your audience and your performance remains unbeatable.

I was asked this question during my public speaking workshop recently by a participant; Sherry what is important – rehearsing your talk well or Spontaneity?

I knew he wanted me to answer – Spontaneity :)

In the capacity of a public speaking coach, I replied this way –

"Rehearsals help you create your prime form of spontaneity."

CHAPTER THREE

HOW TO MASTER PUBLIC SPEAKING?

"Only the prepared speaker deserves to be confident."

—Dale Carnegie

HOW TO LEARN PUBLIC SPEAKING AND MASTER IT

The biggest advantage in public speaking is you always know what will happen next as a public speaker. And if you are a public speaker you are always in the spotlight as a celebrity.

But it is not so easy to be a public speaker, preparing your toasts and influencing an audience.

From where to learn; many people have this question in mind.

I'll give you my helicopter view.

TOASTMASTERS INTERNATIONAL

They have clubs in your vicinity, check it out. I feel the best way for a common to learn and hone speaking skills is to speak regularly. But it's a journey here not a sprint and I have personally met many toastmasters who feel lack of guidance or felt stuck in politics after a certain level achieved. If you are a beginner or have a student-approach in life, there is no harm joining any time.

THEATRE

If you love mimicking actors or you are fond of showing your talent or had this fantasy of becoming a professional actor, this skill can help you big time in your speaking.

In fact, theatre is a great way to learn the art of public speaking. One of my dear friends Major Mohommed Ali Shah is a great example. Being into the theatre for some time and actor in some hit movies, he is now working as a successful motivational speaker with one of the highest TEDx talk givers in the country. Remember background matters. If you have a theatre exposure and reading my book, I just shared a pro tip for you.

MS TALKS INDIA

I couldn't find any such platform so I created one in 2017. We do talk shows, public speaking conferences and workshops across pan India. I believe in giving an opportunity to a common man. Join MS Talks and become a public speaker. We have a tagline 'Inspiration from anywhere' and we as a team live that every day. MS Talks helps you live your dream, hone your skills, meet fellow public speakers and brand yourself as a speaker. Try us (:

FIND A MENTOR

Achrekar used to make Sachin ride with him on his scooter and take him to matches to give the young boy plenty of exposure to cricket. And the coach always placed a one- rupee coin on the stumps while coaching Tendulkar. If he was able to bat through the entire session without being dismissed, he would give Tendulkar the coin. Even today, Sachin has 13 of those precious coins as a part of his treasure trove.

Virat Kohli never forgets to drop a wish or make a call to Sharma on Teacher's Day but 2014 was different. His brother's arrival at his house so early in the day was the cause for concern. Vikas stepped into the house, dialed a number and handed his cell phone to Raj Kumar and Virat said, "Sir - I can't give you back what you have given me in life but a small gift outside is waiting for you," and it was a brand new Skoda car.

I am emphasizing the importance of mentor here even if you are at the pinnacle of your profession. Never underestimate that. A mentor is a person who can see something in you which you cannot see at times. As I always say, I am no public speaking expert, I am an expert public speaking student.

WHY KNOWING ONESELF IS IMPORTANT FOR A PUBLIC SPEAKER?

Aristotle says," Knowing yourself is the beginning of all wisdom."

I always emphasize in my speeches how much you care and love yourself is what will decide your personal dimension. Do you value self-care?

This is one of the deciding factors to become a public speaker and doing public speaking to deliver an effective speech in your niche and domain.

Self-care includes all the things you do to take care of your well-being in four key dimensions: your emotional, physical, psychological and spiritual health.

Your flow of talk is strongly connected to your thoughts, ability to speak and how true you are to yourself on the day when you speak.

It has a great impact on your speaking and transformation.

In speech coaching sessions I follow this practice with my mentees and it has helped them knowing their self- care key dimensions.

Even Les Brown, the no.1 motivational speaker had public speaking fear.

Here is an excerpt from his famous interview;

Interviewer: How did you overcome your aversion to public speaking?

Les Brown: I knew I was good in small groups, but I could not bring myself to think and to speak and to be confident before a large audience. I met a speaker named Mike Williams, who is my mentor to this day. I told him, "I'll give anything to speak like you." He said,

"I'll teach you." And he taught me.

Because of Mike's teaching, I've gone from speaking to one person to speaking to more than 80,000 people in the Georgia Dome.

Mike helped me to begin to recognize and conquer my inner restriction. I would just freeze when I would stand before a larger audience. My mind would be empty.

In fact, at the Georgia Dome, I made the mistake of looking out at the audience before going out on stage. Then I ran and hid in a restroom. My friend Dexter Yager came to the restroom and said, "Brown, are you all right?" And I said, "No. I have to get myself together." He said, "The band is stalling. They need you to come out. We want to introduce you."

Then my mentor, Mike, said, "Man, come out of the bathroom." I said, "I can't, Mike. I don't know what to say. My mind is empty. I can't think. My heart is beating really fast. I'm having shortness of breath."

Mike said, "Brown, are you scared?" I said, "Yes." He said, "Brown, listen to me. They came to see you. You didn't come to see them. All I'm asking you to do is get the microphone, maintain eye contact with me, and pretend you're in your living room. I'll be down front."

So, when I came out of the restroom and we're walking toward the stage, I said, "Will somebody pray for me?" And so they stopped, and they prayed for me. Then I remember going up the steps and somebody asked, "Do you think he's going to be all right?" And Mike said, "Yes. He's going to be just fine."

I went up and gave a speech called "It's Not Over Until I Win," and that has become the biggest seller in the history of speeches. That speech was driven by fear.

I have written this book with all my real experience and knowledge. There is still more to come. Public Speaking is a deep well. I realized this when I started learning more and more as a speaker.

Out of the millions of speeches delivered each day, only a small percentage are delivered well.

This book is not a roadmap for becoming a public speaker. Obviously, everyone has its own style of speaking and understanding, but you will read and learn which I kept on registering in my mind through my own experiential journey of public speaking and now decided to share it with the world.

SPEECH STRUCTURE AND TYPES

Speech body is mainly divided into three parts:

Introduction: You need to gain the audience's attention, engage the listeners and always stay connected to the core message of your speech.

Body: Information part. It contains approximately 75-80% portion of your speech. What you will speak, all the main points clearly stated and supported by anecdotes, practical examples, supporting material and research.

Conclusion: Review your main points and provides closure by ending with a conclusion and call to action for the audience again connecting to the core message of your speech.

TYPES OF SPEECHES

Workshop / Informative Speech / Oral Report / Lecture: Designed to define, clarify, compare, explain, instruct, demonstrate and teach.

Persuasive speech/debates/sales presentations/sermons: Spoken to inspire, influence, convince, sell products and services, preach or pushing for a particular action.

Evocative speech: Stand-up comedy, celebration talks, help the audience to enjoy like the office party or a birthday/family gathering, bond, toast or commemorate.

Impromptu Speech: To speak on the spur on any topic. Follow F.A.T. method Feel- Anecdote-Tie back. Feel how you feel about the situation, share an anecdote and tie it with the situation towards the end.

Eulogy: Speech given at temples when someone passes away or at a funeral. Introduce, share a deeply personal speech, show your concern about the person passed away, thank attendees, show gratitude towards all.

The Storytelling Speech: Pick stories to connect. It helps in creating a zone of quick common understanding using experiences, goals, beliefs, transformation to persuade for action.

FEW STRUCTURES & IDEAS FOR SPEECHES AND TALKS

- Talk about something which can create drama and tension in the audience and then speak on the solutions. Problem followed by a solution

- Ask your audience. Let them attempt wrong and this way your audience connect will be superior.

- Let the audience anticipate. I use this the most if I have a post-lunch session wherein the audience feels sleepy.

- Story – Talk – Story- Talk – Call to action- End of talk

- Talk-audience Q&A- Talk-Stories-Activity-Talk-Let Audience Network-Talk-Call to action- End of talk

- Talk- Trivia-Stories-Trivia – Talk – Stories – Call to action- End of talk

- Talks – Trivia – Solve a Problem-Talk –Stories – Talks – Call to action – End of talk

You can create your right mix as per your choice. Every audience interaction is different, so interaction may go against you. However, if you feel like a subject matter expert, it is one of the best structures of public speaking. I have seen Arfeen Khan – Life coach from India doing that live in the audience. That to me is gutsy and authentic.

CHAPTER FOUR

HOW TO OVERCOME STAGE FEAR - 2 STRATEGIES REVEALED?

"Death is the number two fear that people have and public speaking is the first!"

—Sidney Sheldon

In 2007, while serving a job in a corporate as a manager I was in a relationship with a kind-hearted girl and her name was Jasmine.

I and my girlfriend Jasmine were in the car. She was wearing her green color velvet suit and was looking gorgeous. We kissed each other, she was happier than me because I was about to receive a big award for the first time in my life. Though we couldn't marry each other later on.

I was a shy person during my entire school life. I was teased by many students and classmates around who now follow me as an International Influencer.

In 2007, while I was serving a private bank group, I got nominated for the best relationship manager of the year award amongst 200 top managers in the country.

The Country head announced my name and I got thunderous applause from everyone. And I was asked to share my experience as to how I achieve such big targets and the strategy around. when I came near to dais podium, I couldn't convey anything except my smile.

In fact, I wanted to run from that place.

Butterflies are funny. Some days they make you feel dumb on stage, some days they make you run to the toilet, other days they make you horny.*

Historically, the first-ever panic attack, which I realized later- it was. And I walked down the stage avoiding saying about my own success story. I was annoyed and devastated by this.

But, I did pledge to overcome the fear of public speaking and make my name.

Since then I have researched many modalities to remove stage fear and used it with my mentees but I am not highlighting all of them here. I am sharing two simple strategies that anyone can apply to overcome stage fear.

STRATEGY NO.1: SYSTEMATIC DESENSITIZATION

Understand this term carefully before you follow it. Go deep into it and that's what I did and I changed the way of public speaking for myself.

I followed **Systematic Desensitization** which is a behavioral psychology technique meaning *repetition till you improve* and works well in removing public speaking fear-

It all started with first free 30 speeches with students in academies.

And then no looking back ladies and gentlemen.

And this led me to my career transformation from a banker to a corporate trainer and now one of the renowned public speaking coaches in India.

In 2017, I gave myself a realistic target of 100 professional speeches in the next 3 years and I have already achieved 150+ speeches and spoke on the prestigious platforms of India which includes 3 TEDx talks and 3 Josh talks last year in different languages.

It's a dream of our parents to educate their kids in a top educational institution of India.

Even a bigger dream for a 'speaker' is to speak at such a top institution with a full packed audience in an auditorium.

I take deep pride and gratitude in sharing that a boy who was struggling for his own studies in childhood due to financial crunch in the family is now going to address his talk at one of the most prominent institutes of India.

I will be talking in front of IIT college students and staff members at Kharagpur.

(Please watch my josh talks video to get more clarity on my real story.)*

Josh talks link: *https://www.youtube.com/watch?v=3xbk 66qeh8I&t=66s*

I am formally confirmed and invited for my 4th TEDx talk at IIT Kharagpur in March, 2020.

This includes my several interviews with national media and local TV channels. I have appeared on more than 30 times in various media interviews, talks and done a few conferences as emcee now.

Unbelievable, how did I achieve this, from where I was?

Talk as much as you can. You will find your flow. A simple and natural biological process is our development of the brain. That's why you see some kids are overwhelming in public speaking. Is it God gifted? No. They reached the desensitize level early due to less garbage in the brain that helped them to focus. Your brain synapses are activated to produce content, to think and speak on your feet. Once your speaking synapses are active in your brain, nothing is stopping you if you work with all your capacity, strength and sagacity, faith, hope, confidence, stern pertinacity.

If you want to overcome social anxiety, be more social.

If you want to speak in public, go to public events more. Network with people. Notice how they talk, present and connect. This book is the best result of it. I had attended more than 250+ workshops, events in the last 5 and half years offline, online included. It has a greater impact on me.

I surrounded myself with some finest speakers who are doing what I wanted to do. And eventually, I got better in my profession and doing what I saw them doing, in fact, a step ahead from many of them.

Through my brand MS Talks India, I am on a mission to create 1 million public speakers in India by 2030.

STRATEGY NO.2: RE-APPRISE YOUR FEAR INTO EXCITEMENT

In public speaking, remain in anxiety and speak anyway. Don't know how this works inside but as you speak a bit, gradually fear evades.

Fear is an aroused physiological state which is characteristic of both stress and pleasure.

Harvard research studies by Alison wood in 2013 has proven it.

Since both fear and excitement have the same physiological state, all you need to do is to re-apprise your fear into excitement.

Stress is connected to your fear and pleasure is to excitement.

My point is that parts of your body will respond in ancient ways to stress, no matter how prepared you are. That's OK. It doesn't mean you're weird or a coward, it just means your body is trying hard to save your life.

It's nice of your body to do this, in the same way, **it's nice of your dog to protect you** from squirrels. It's hard to blame a dog for its instinctive behavior, and the same understanding should be applied to your own brain.[*]

If you have a public speaking fear, remain in anxiety and speak anyway and that's where you will stand in the light and be seen as you are.

---

[*]Confessions of a public speaker – Scott Berkun

CHAPTER FIVE

RE-PUBLIC SPEAKING

"You cannot speak that which you do not know. You cannot share that which you do not feel. You cannot translate that which you do not have. And you cannot give that which you do not possess. To give it and to share it, and for it to be effective, you first need to have it."

—Jim Rohn

The word **republic** comes from the Latin language words res publica, which **means** a "public thing". Public speaking is a public thing.

That means you first need to live what you teach. That's an important tip to note. I live and learn more by giving speeches, it gives me the empowerment. I get to know more about the market.

To understand how public speaking works lets understand the perspective of an audience and public speaker;

HOW AUDIENCE THINK ABOUT A SPEAKER?

1. Can a speaker really teach me and is he worth the topic?

2. Will a speaker be able to influence the public in the hall?

3. Does a speaker have effective skills to communicate?

HOW A SPEAKER THINK ABOUT AN AUDIENCE?

1. How can I connect with all?

2. What do I want them to know?

3. What do I want them to do?

In fact, your attitude often overpowers the words you use when speaking to others. The exact words that you use are sometimes far less important than the energy, intensity, and conviction with which you use them. I give webinars and training sessions to a lot of trainees every month and do personal coaching too. I have found out that even if they are attending my online session from a distant place they feel the warmth when I speak and explain the things to them. It's true in my case. This is similar when you talk to your friends, relatives from India to Canada, United States, or any other country. People may hear your words, but they always feel your attitude.

Let me make it more clear with an example:

I am sure you drive a car or have seen a lot of people driving cars around you;

It looks so simple but a lot of things are expected to be regular and effective for a smooth drive of car on the road.

A car should have oil, engine, steering, horn, brakes and many such important parts to run on the road. Everything goes together to make the car have a fluent run.

Art of public speaking is very much like how a car gets ready to launch on the road..

The art of communicating beyond words requires the ability to bring all four of those factors together—using the right words with the exact emotion while being intellectually convincing and making the right visual impression. And all this needs to be done with the right tone of voice, the right facial expressions, and positive body language.

I know this sounds complicated. And it is. But it's also intuitive.

I want to make clear today that in almost domain we are surrounded by public speakers and influencers who have so much to teach you.

SECTION TWO
PRACTICE

CHAPTER SIX

WHAT'S IN IT FOR THE AUDIENCE?

"When presenting a speech, don't think about how audience will look at you. Think about what value you can give them."

—Synonymous

Every speaker love to create an experience for their audience. When we do talk about a speaker's primary role to move the audience it starts and ends with only one thing – WIIFA- *What's In It for Audience?*

WHAT'S IN IT FOR THE AUDIENCE?

Great speakers know that it's all about the audience. If the audience doesn't get the message, the job is not done. The same is true of keynoting. Nonetheless, some speakers do want to involve the audience much. They love to do it in a much more tightly controlled and circumscribed way. I'm a huge fan of getting the audience to perform and do things with me as a speaker, even in keynotes. But I'm keenly aware that it's harder to play by the keynoting rules. You have to get good at creating rapport instantly so that your audience will feel comfortable participating and got to position yourself well to control your inputs so that you can get your keynote accomplished.

NATURAL FLOW

If I ask you, do you ask yourself to breathe in out, in out... No, you don't. It comes naturally to you. It is without already having planned. Best example: a cricket batsman hitting the ball, he uses his instinct. Improvising your spontaneity in public speaking is going without a script and talking about what you already have fed in your brain through experiences of life known as impromptu speaking.

Natural flows help in remaining audience-centric.

Why? Because people want to listen to a person who is like him or her. That's it.

Don't presume or behave like you are over smart. Be smart and people-friendly.

The audience appreciates that more.

NOVELTY

The best speakers are always finding ways to deliver information in new ways.

Let me ask you;

Did you ever have an urge to meditate, listen to your favorite music, go for running or follow a fitness regime at the gym?

What will be your answer with respect to neuroscience? Think....Think

Here is the neurological perspective; it is because you receive a sudden increase in your dopamine levels inside the brain doing all these activities.

Apart from meditation, listening to cool music, exercise, the 'enthusiasm' increases the dopamine levels immediately.

Here is the connection for you as a speaker now,

If you can bring novelty to your speech, you can bring enthusiasm instantly.

You are a winner for the audience. Almost all the famous speeches of all time have novelty.

The human brain loves novelty. An unfamiliar, unusual, or unexpected element in a presentation intrigues the audience, jolts them out of their preconceived notions, and quickly gives them a new way of looking at the world.[*]

HOW TO SPARK ON STAGE

Don't go far, the best example is Tony Robbins, an author, speaker and life coach.

Someone close to him told me about Tony's schedule.

"Tony Robbins has a pre-speech ritual that he always follows. This preparation starts hours before he arrives at the venue. Robbins starts his mornings with a dip into a cold pool. The aim is to wake his body up and get his mind whirring as quickly as possible.

Once he's at the venue, he has another set of rituals. Robbins performs an array of breathing and voice exercises. He meditates and he even has a trampoline that he bounces on before hitting the stage. All of this prepares his mind and body for the performance. And it is through the energy that he injects into his performance that he's able to influence people."

The audience doesn't like speakers who are only well-rehearsed and don't use spontaneity,

---

*Talk like TED – Carmine Gallo

Neither they like speakers who are only spontaneous but are not rehearsed.

When you are on the podium, you are a performer. If you feel good about what you are doing any which ways you will end up stunning your audience and putting up a remarkable show. Your energy vibrations always reach your audience apart from your gestures, content and everything else.

Be audience-centric. That's a leap for public speaking.

CHAPTER SEVEN

HOW TO USE PROP AS A PUBLIC SPEAKER?

"Props can add an impeccable impact on your presentation."

—Author Sherry

'Prop' is a short word to "property" which is used by speakers around the globe on the stage.

I have encouraged many different props at International Public Speaking Championship (IPSC) held in Gurugram, India on December 21, 2019, where 30 speakers participated in a day organized by my company MS Talks India. We invited Philippa Mathewson an International Trainer, Co-founder and Director Tranziam joined with 3 other experts on the Jury panel.

I curated this event where there was an age group limit from 12 years to 70 years with a prop usage kept as mandatory.

WHY PROP IN PUBLIC SPEAKING?

Props help your audience to excite and arouse interest when you do a public speaking engagement. The prop can be used as a substitute for notes. Prop helps focusing the attention on the speaking points you are trying to make along with illustrating them for you. They make better connections than your words with the visually oriented members of your audience. Prop creates enthusiasm in the audience, adds variety to your delivery of talk and makes your points more memorable.

DIFFERENT TYPES OF PROPS

- Flower or bunch of flowers
- Fruit, Vegetable
- Mirror
- Snakes & ladders board
- Ball/cap/keys
- Balloon float or burst
- Bunch of papers
- Bin with a surprise
- Fire ignite through match-box
- A cigarette
- A rope or threads
- Colorful frames or painting

TIPS FOR USING PROPS

- Normally you should keep your special props hidden until you are ready to use them to bring excitement in the room. That's essential in public speaking.
- Make sure the prop can be seen from all parts of the room and the audience can connect in one glance.
- Don't make this mistake to avoid an audience. Always speak to the audience, not the prop (unless the prop is a puppet).

- In general, you should only use the prop if it's actually required there to put forward a strong point or for any critical explanation, else avoid it. It can spoil a talk too.

- Make sure the audience is focused on surprise props before you unleash the surprise. (If using a fake peanut can with pop out snakes, hold the can in full view for an extra second before you open it so the audience does not miss it).

Take the expertise of a public speaking coach if you want to use 'prop' for a special talk on a platform for any special day. It is not so easy as it requires preparation and content alignment. I remember I once used "an apple" as a prop at MS Talks while anchoring and forgot my script. I concluded I was not prepared well. Your alignment is crucial.

Watch world championship of public speaking organized by toastmasters international and you will get a good idea of prop usage. It has a lot of videos on YouTube with prop usage by a speaker for public speaking.

I attempted a thermocol made human skull as a prop in a TEDx Talk happened in January 2020.

CHAPTER EIGHT

ROLE OF STORYTELLING IN PUBLIC SPEAKING

*"Listeners want to be engaged and entertained and
that hasn't changed for thousands of years."*

—Carmine Gallo

As a public speaker one of the best experiences will eventuate when you speak for a few hours, you are all together in a different zone. A level up from the audience. The more you speak, the more you align yourself with the right energy and refined content of your mind and that never fails to impress the audience. The audience feels zapped with your intensity and consistency of sharing. And the story is the most powerful tool in your arsenal. The story in public speaking helps you to command that winning zone for you as a public speaker. It is so easy to impress the audience. But how to do that, let's find out.

ROLE OF STORYTELLING IN PUBLIC SPEAKING

Around you the concept of storytelling prevails - movies, newspapers, news channels, books, you are surrounded by the stories.

The audience loves the stories which have ups and downs, truth or betrayal, we as human beings are brain-wired to it.

I have found that no matter what expertise you have, no matter how much skill you might carry, I can find out more about that online on the internet. Sam Cawthorn an Australian motivational speaker says, 'One thing that I have realized is that your greatest ever trump card is your story. It's your only secret weapon and unique value proposition to every other person on the planet.'

One of my friend Praveen Wadalkar, International storyteller & 6 times TEDx speaker and MS Talks speaker once told me,

"Sherry - No matter how much information, expertise or knowledge that you might have it no longer is good enough, what we need to do is we need to learn how to tell our stories. We don't know how to present our stories. When I realized it, I have learned it from experts".

It hit me like a tornado. Man! He is damn right.

At MS Talks, we invite people to share their real-life stories and experiences.

One of the keynote speakers at MS Talks - Mr. Dinesh Mohan (Bollywood actor, supermodel) shared his journey on how someone who couldn't walk for 8 months is now walking for premium brands. Dinesh became a supermodel and actor at the age of 57.

He was outstanding in his spontaneity and speech delivery in less than 15 minutes of talk. Also, he won a special storytelling award for the best story by the award-winning author – *Jolly Uncle, himself a great storyteller, motivational writer.*

There are few human beings you always remember; they make a mark on your mind.

I know some people in my network who while in a normal conversation with me, intensify their talk through smile, intonation and positive thinking.

Stories that are well narrated transport soul to the normal talk we usually do.

Being a great storyteller makes you feel more confident, persuasive and helps the audience absorb a key point. Best public speakers have mastered the art of storytelling too. This art can be learned by avid listening, speaking, reading and rehearsing. It's all about your hunger to learn and improvise. Listening and reading different stories helps you to create a model of your stories which you can use it in your keynotes or talks.

The art of storytelling is a strategic tool used in business communication, branding, recalling of brand value and other key services. The corporate world and business tycoons in India and abroad have realized the potential of storytelling.

We homo-sapiens are brain-wired from inside to get attracted to stories. *Remember your childhood, Dadi maa (grandmother) tales, Daadu (grandfather) jungle stories* – We all have those memories to cherish.

Storytelling is the most effective tool which can do the mind shift of the audience to take the action.

WHY USE STORYTELLING IN PUBLIC SPEAKING

The most important skill to reach the heart and minds of people is Storytelling. I have seen and listened to many public speakers mastering this art and I am also in the learning phase. Everyone communicates, but how one does storytelling makes all the difference.

- *Storytelling is one of the best tools to communicate your message and empower your audience.*

- *Storytelling helps recall already stored information in the mind easily, due to the power of cognitive thinking, auditory cortex and sensory associations.*

- *Storytelling fascinates an individual to create visuals inside your brain.*

- *Storytelling connects you to the reservoir in sub- conscious by gaining access to your personal experiences and the concept clarification in a most amenable way by activating multiples senses in the brain.*

- *Storytelling helps in engaging the audience using humor too by simply reversing what the audience was expecting on a certain point. And you can make them laugh easily.*

Question: *When you grow up, why do you love to interact with your mom, dad, sister, brother about your actions and habits in childhood?*

Answer: *It has a story; you love your story.*

STORIES ARE POWERFUL

Take a reverse case first. When the brain is not making any effort, it requires an intervention that is really boring and senseless. A bed sleep rhyme is a great metaphor so as a novel read which helps to separate stress of the day. In short, delta (deep sleep) brain waves are formed.

If you are an insomniac, bedtime stories are intentionally created in a boring way by story writers that in no time you start yawning and fall asleep. It is like you don't' drink alcohol but your drunken friend is talking so much and to avoid the conversation, you pick the bed sheet to cover the face and start snoring.

Stories have the power to do a paradigm shift of mind from one pattern to another.

But how?

Most of the speakers do storytelling in such a way that it forms a brain wave shift of the listeners. Alpha to Beta is the route. Sometimes it is really quick and I mean it.

It is important to understand the frequency of **brain-waves* below:

Delta 0.5Hz–4Hz - Deep sleep

Theta 4Hz–8Hz - Drowsiness (also first stage of sleep)

Alpha 8Hz–14Hz - Relaxed but alert

Beta 14Hz–30Hz - Highly alert and focused

In reality, storytelling helps to switch on the delta (deep sleep) or beta (alertness, focus) both.

In a normal case, as a public speaker, we need **beta** the most at the audience end.

Great leaders, thinkers, influencers and public speakers know the significance of stories.

Question: *Why do you love lengthy talking with friends?*

Answer: *It has stories and we love to connect and know about friends through storytelling.*

---

*Brain-waves - Different sources provide different frequency values, these are average Hz's.

THE KURT VONNEGUT STRATEGY

I call this strategy by his name after a deep understanding of the video I saw.

Kurt has spent over 5 decades in writing novels and storytelling.

Kurt explains the ideas of sharing your story. Every story you see has a range.

BROADLY THREE RANGES

(a) Individuals getting in trouble – gets out of trouble – People love that story.

(b) Life was really good- life got worse – got it back again in life – People like that story.

(c) Life is Low – someone helped – life is at high – again a steep downfall – then getting everything back and achieving happiness – People love the beautiful ending.

Here is the full video: *https://www.youtube.com/results?search_query=kurt+vonnegut*

Oprah Winfrey Strategy: If you listen closely to Oprah Winfrey; as a storyteller, Oprah uses a classic narrative technique to inspire her audience:

- Start with humble beginnings.
- Help your audience see themselves in the story.
- Turn the experience into a lesson.

'STEP' STORYTELLING APPROACH

Being an expert student of public speaking, I have learned different structures and techniques which I use in story-telling. I am keeping it simple here.

Structure: What is in it for the audience? Connect the key point to the moral of your story. It has to be directionally connecting to a key takeaway. Make a story using appropriate words and phrases best suited for your audience type.

Truthfulness: Share a story that has stirred you from inside first, only then you would be able to connect with authenticity and high energy. Another best way is by talking about your own failures and struggles; you make an emotional connection with your audience.

Emotion: Remember, you are talking to human beings, without emotions you would hardly gain thought access in the audience's brain. Use it with the utmost awareness.

Perform: Perform as if you are in characters of your story, use popular names. Filmy names like *Jai, Veeru, Khan chacha (Indian audience connects really well to such names).*

Hey! Just examples, as I said make it appealing to perform your best.

It's completely your choice. I know you will decide the best.

Your content is the easy part. But when it comes to the performance, effectiveness to show a story rather than just telling it is what matters the most. It is all about connecting with the listeners and taking them on a memorable journey

Lisa Nicholas, New York Times bestselling author, a millionaire entrepreneur and a motivational speaker believes that rather telling the story, you must show your story. By showing the story she means – you express through robust actions to captivate your audience. Imbibe yourself so much into it that the audience rides on the feelings you want them to ride upon.

Authentic storytelling should come from inside you.

As a storyteller, you are unclad in front of your audience. Have the courage to show your vulnerability and you will touch that precise learning part of the listener.

I just shared a few workable storytelling techniques from the many strategies I have learnt from renowned speakers and my mentors.

I am not born with storytelling finesse; it is a skill I have learned.

I consider myself an amateur in this area, but regardless of your background, I think you should evaluate what moves your audience and make changes you want to make in this vital area.

Never underestimate stories.

CHAPTER NINE

CONQUER SOCIAL ANXIETY AND PANIC ATTACKS

"To understand your fear is the beginning of really seeing."

—Bruce Lee

Social anxiety disorder happens to you when everyday interactions cause significant worry and self-consciousness because you fear of being judged by others.

According to studies, like certain illnesses, such as diabetes, anxiety disorders, attacks are caused by chemical imbalances in the body. Studies have shown that severe or long-lasting stress can change the balance of chemicals in the brain that controls mood.

Human beings are wired for fears. If your body is in motion you will create emotions.

Fear is an emotion. That's right!

What is even more frightening is that social anxiety when mixed with negative emotion creates an unstable situation and you end up doing the mistake of accepting your anxiety as a reality and get lost somewhere. It takes time to come out and by the time you recover, the damage had been done.

The emotion of fear is controlled by *the amygdala.*

Amygdala is linked to the parts of the brain that govern your senses, muscles, and hormones – enabling your body to react quickly to the sight or sound of a threat that causes different emotions like anxiety, fear, happiness, excitement, power of possibility.

Due to their interrelation, fear causes anxiety and anxiety can cause fear.

Breathing with proper oxygen supply in the entire body and meditation can help you cure this problem with magical results.

Hey, I am not a science geek! I am just a speaking coach :)

But, if you deep dive into the root levels, the biggest challenge in public speaking is the fear of speaking on the podium. Shockingly, it is one of the topmost phobias in the world.

Glossophobia is the name of the phobia causing fear of public speaking.

Now, going by the logic that humans are wired for fears, we have to accept it.

Hello! Accept it. Yes, I am telling you.

Believe it or not, phobias are part of our lives.

Here are a few phobias which I have observed amongst people around me;

1. *Arachnophobia*: The fear of spiders affects women four times more. (*48% women and 12% men*)

2. *Agoraphobia:* The fear of open or crowded spaces.

3. *Cynophobia:* The fear of dogs.

4. *Cherophobia:* The fear of happiness,

5. *Anthropophobia:* Pathological fear of people or human company.

6. *Didaskaleinophobia:* Fear of going to school.

7. *Acrophobia:* Fear of heights.

8. *Glossophobia:* Speech anxiety or fear of public speaking.

Check the Top 100 phobias of the world here: **https://www. fearof.net/**

I suggest you need to change your physiology to change your mind and situations around you. A mentor can help big time or a strong emotional feeling to get back in your soul mode is a powerful solution. But it's not so easy.

In one of the TEDx events organized by Delhi Technical University, New Delhi India a few years back, I witnessed and met one of the speakers - Ms. Sandra Colhando, an English Honors from Delhi University & Leadership coach. She confessed in her talk, *"My life was miserable until I did sky jumping to get rid of fear and transformed my life."*

Fear and panic exist but so do solutions. It depends on how you feel about overcoming it and what actions you are ready to take in your life.

For public speaking while you are called at the podium, you can note and try to apply this formula of **AWARE** to quickly change your notions;

A - accept the fear, don't try to brawl.

W - watch the fear, breathe in and out with full force at least 5 times.

A - act normal and smile whenever you can.

R - repeat **AWA** in the mind again to strengthen your confidence.

E - expect the best as a speaker and be proud as you have earned it to speak on the podium.

It will help immensely and you will feel better.

You can overcome social phobia which is a mental disorder.

I firmly believe it is curable and I did that with a couple of my mentees working with me for public speaking coaching to overcome stage fright and social anxiety. I cannot claim it evaporated completely but we did overrule it by having their speeches in full packed room of audience and now they are public speakers.

Public speaking is a journey of fright to might.

CHAPTER TEN

3 TOP TRAITS FOR SPEECH PREPARATION

*"There are only two types of speakers in the world.
1. The nervous and 2. The liars."*

–Mark Twain

Effective public speaking is a critical component of mastering success. By mastering the art of public speaking, you'll increase every level of performance in your personal growth. I've often said that if you just communicate well, you can get by at any leadership profile you are in whether in job or business.

To excel at public speaking you must do more than just overpower your nervous heebie-jeebies.

You must also have confidence in your subject and be yourself while you are on stage.

You must have heard about being authentic but in reality, it is a mix of authenticity & rehearses.

VIDEO CRAFTING

Create your videos when you rehearse and see how you are coming up. You might have heard this earlier. Videos help us in creating a level of concentration and focus we need for our talks. Check your voice throw, range of voice and facial expressions.

Many people say I have a camera phobia. I suggest see into the camera and visualize any moment which makes you feel good and in no time you will see your body and facial expressions changing.

For example: Watch on the mobile camera. Visualize as if you are addressing 100-300 students and suddenly you feel that your body mechanism works totally differently. You will smile more, express more while speaking in front of the camera and create a confident video. Create your own video vault on YouTube. It's all free with a workable internet connection. Once you create your flow with a few videos, you will notice your skills brushing up and you will create your own style to talk. Try this simple technique.

Preparation and rehearsals are the keys to public speaking.

WHAT TO EAT AND DRINK

If it is winter, have a few sips of warm water or if it is summer avoid cold water and prefer a normal one to give comfort to your vocal chords which are going to help you with your talk.

Avoid coffee or any drink which can pump your blood pressure. It's not required before the talk.

Follow meals as per your body. I prefer a hot cup of tea with a couple of cookies generally or vegetable juice or a protein chocolate bar for energy.

If you are speaking for the whole day; Eat light food, have juices if arrangements are there in the venue during breaks or carry on your own. Avoid heavy food and overeating. This will help you to create a great mental balance.

BEST PRACTICES

Always prefer to visit the venue a few days before the talk.

This is specially recommended if you are going for platforms like TEDx if you can accommodate

Follow the basics. For most of the talks, I visit auditorium or venue a week before or sometimes much earlier to get the idea of hall structure, check out the lights, area to stand and speak, the audience sitting arrangement, projector positioning, audio and mic arrangements, etc.

I follow this habit for my key events, workshops and seminars I am involved as a speaker or being an organizer of MS Talks.

When you rehearse with the feel of the venue you will feel an edge on the day of your talk. Also try to practice in sunlight to have real-time sweat, a loud noise of television or music. This will again strengthen you from inside not to skip or forget and manage the real-time disturbance on the day of your talk. You will have mind patterns ready to face any obstruction on the real day.

I always try to reach the venue 30-60 minutes to avoid last-minute rush. This gives me a cushion as a speaker. I interact with the people at the venue, network with them before my talk. Try to understand the taste and personalities I am around. I also attempt to check their expectations wherever I feel possible for the event or talk. This way I get an idea of what can work for me to impress the audience. In the context of public speaking, it's an important tip.

Now to prepare your speech for public speaking, I've got three key traits for you.

HERE THEY ARE

1. Audience first sensitivity: Sharpen your curiosity and your interest in life and people. Those are the big subjects: life and people. The questions you might have about life and the mysteries of life. What about people and human behavior?

What does your audience want to listen to is extremely significant compared to what exactly you want to speak?

The GOOD news is you can learn to speak as per your audience if you know your topic well and you have prepared it.

I heard many of the speakers cocksure, I will be myself when I am in front of the audience, preparation is not my cup of tea.

Well, I can only say it is a big myth. You cannot afford to take it lightly at any level. It is like lifting heavy weights at the gym and expecting the muscle to grow without proper nutrition. *(you will read ahead why rehearsing your speech is crucial)*

The benefit of rehearsed speech is you will be having a ready layer in the mind as you speak because you don't need to worry about what you are going to say next. This avoids the unstoppable mind - chatter and talking in circles because you don't know what is coming next.

Some key aspects for excellent speech delivery and I always make sure to include them:

a. Connecting to yourself first: Ideate about your body positioning to use the podium, eye movements. This is your first step even before connecting to your audience.

b. Knowing your audience age and profile category: The content creation has to be in sync and your ideology will match easily. Speak as an audience advocate.

c. Audience engagement story/excerpt: Make sure it is connected to the central idea of your speech. Transport the audience to the scene. Don't report a dialogue, deliver a dialogue.

d. Proper preparation of speech please: Studies show that preparation can reduce your fear by 80%. The more prepared you are the fewer nervous you will be, before and while speaking in front of the audience. Record every presentation and look at it from your audience's perspective.

2. Fascination: Go from interested to fascinate. Interested people want to know - *Does it work?* Fascinated people want to know - *How does it work?*

I was invited to for a keynote at a business community where I spoke on the topic - "How to grow more confidence in life?"

The profile of my audience was elite entrepreneurs and top corporate executives of Delhi/NCR.

I was completely fascinated to give top learning from my talk to the audience and I did an activity which was appreciated by everyone.

> *"I was talking about 'Progress' as one of the key pointers*
> *to achieve more confidence in life."*

Progress comes from success, success comes from confidence, confidence comes from action and action comes from self-talks.

After the context setting about 'progress'; I commenced the activity.

I requested the audience to close the eyes and visualize a major goal.

I motivated them –'Hope you will achieve it one day.'

Hope! Hope! Hope! Hope! Hope!

Then I requested everyone to shift the state of mind and visualize about a major goal:

Now, I motivated them –'You will definitely achieve it.'

Definitely! Definitely! Definitely! Definitely! Definitely!

Stop!!! Open your eyes.

Did you feel any change in your body and the way you have visualized - Hope versus definiteness of goal achievement in mind?

Everyone admitted that when we were hoping during visualization the pictures in our mind were a blur, unclear vis-a-vis when we changed our state of mind to definitely achieve the goal, the pictures during visualization were almost clear and visible which helps create confidence instantaneously. Confidence is something we don't have, it is something we create and we can create it any moment of time.

Explaining 'how' will add credibility and authenticity to your talk. Conceptualize what can fascinate the audience and the ideas coming your way can actually amaze you and your speech can become worthy of a standing ovation.

3. Subject knowledge: So we have got sensitivity and we have got fascination, Here's one more word: *knowledge.* You just have to know. Collect knowledge in your notes from the things you observe and the stuff you read, from your ongoing education. Presently, I record all my stories, ideas, thoughts and synopsis from books in the Evernote app and Google Keep.

Fill up your mental, spiritual and emotional bank enough so that it becomes like an unending reservoir to draw from. That begins to help you prepare. Do your research. Gather up stories. Keep the flow of knowledge going into your journal, as well as into your head and into your heart.

Since public speaking has become an eminent part of our lives, I encourage all of you to go and attend workshops, listen to speakers, read and follow different experts which can help inspire you to become your best version of a public speaker.

SECTION THREE
PRESENT

CHAPTER ELEVEN

HOW TO INVOLVE THE AUDIENCE WHEN YOU SPEAK?

"There is only one excuse for a speaker's asking the attention of his audience: he must have either truth or entertainment for them."

—Dale Carnegie, *The Art of Public Speaking*

The easiest way to involve the audience is to talk to your audience in a familiar language. You have to fit in the comfort of your listener's mind. Your audience has to accept you. You can feel that easily by getting the response from the audience. Here a few points;

- The way the audience applauds and expresses on your opinions.
- Getting their nod to your questions and statements.
- Simply seeing their submission through eye-contact.

Yes! You can also do it at ease by knowing how you, as a speaker, can involve the audience on the podium without any hesitation and you must identify what you are good at. That's your niche.

- Relationship & life coaching
- Business growth
- Information Technology
- Communication
- Mindfulness
- Motivational speaking
- Supply chain
- Personality development
- Principles of leadership

or some other topic you can speak well on.

I got a question for you now- How do you find that someone is interested in your talks or not?

Any guesses?

Here is an inside wire - try to speak on different podiums *to create your flow first, niche comes later.*

We all have something best or unique to express. Identify that element and work on your best. Speak at different assignments wherever possible. Be flexible to accept all types of oratory opportunities especially when you are in the beginning phase as a speaker because you are literally exploring yourself.

In a content creative world where internet is available to access all types of content and events, there are several platforms that permits you as an orator like poetry platforms, storytelling open mic, stand up-comedy, public speaking conference seminars and the list is unending. These events are happening around in different cities nearby you.

Opportunities like never before are there in India. Find what suits you. Grab it. In my recent meeting and conversation with Dr. Jaspal Singh ex vice-chancellor, Punjabi University, Patiala he confessed, "Public speaking comes through practice, experience and training. In fact, some speakers acquire the skills naturally by speaking a few times. You only need to figure out where you can improve more and start building yourself in that area and from there you start improving."

Reading relevant books also helps you create positive thoughts and deactivate the blockages of mind created in the past.

If you want the audience to involve in your talks these powerful hacks will help.

Are you ready? Let's go and light a fire.

1. Easiness in language: There is a misconception that communication skills mean 'English speaking'. Wrong. Totally wrong. If you are good at Hindi, make your Hindi vocabulary strong. Don't be in the middle of Hindi or English.

Communication means any language which makes your message easy to understand and inspire others to learn. Let me ask you if I would have chosen with typical glossary words, I would have missed out on many who want to read my write-up in simple English language. The point I am driving home is involvement.

I intentionally use easy words to convey a clear and precise message. This is known as communication. It is imperative to understand that writing and speaking are two different forms of communication. The choice of words makes all the difference because most of us have grown up understanding simple English.

In India, unless it is a niche crowd or you know the audience well, never ever use tough vocabulary just to impress the audience. It may go against you.

2. Personal Story: Talk about your childhood, school days, how you grew up, your mother, father, grandparents. These are so powerful topics to begin the talk that you will be amazed at how quickly people adapt a situation relating it to their lives. Consequently, one of the best ways to involve the audience is to get their yes and involve them in an emotional journey. We all had been through this journey in some or the other way.

Bryan Stevenson, the speaker who earned the longest standing ovation in *TED history, spent 65 percent of his presentation telling stories. He admitted that in my talks often I talk about family members because most of us have family members that we have a relationship to. I talk about kids and people who are vulnerable or struggling. All of those narratives are designed to help understand the issues.

https://www.ted.com/talks/bryan_stevenson_we_need_to_talk_about_an_injustice

3. Curiosity: Let me share an incident with your permission: One fine day, after dawn I was walking in the garden nearby my house and I heard the noise of some heavy thing falling down from a tree. I was frightened, I could barely move and started sweating more. After looking around I gather courage and went ahead to check what was the noise about. What I saw next completely threatened me. It was a dead body of an unidentified old man and his face was bleeding. I was about to collapse and was in complete fear. I ran away from the garden with all possible strength I could gather to reach a lively place. Eventually, I reached a shop nearby to purchase a water bottle.

Staggered! I just created this story to create curiosity for you. Don't bother it is unreal.

Let me share a true story now;

Almost every television thriller shows like Savdhaan India, Gumrah - End of Innocence, Crime Patrol they start the first 1-2 minutes' scenes of their episode the similar way I started the dead man story. They involve you as viewers and many times you don't feel like changing the television channel. Isn't it?

Curiosity can bring you back in the spotlight as a speaker. If anytime you need to involve the audience just make sure some part of your presentation in the starting, middle or end should have this tool included. Again, it completely depends on the theme of presentation but almost it works everywhere.

4. Oxygen of Oration - sweet words: Sweet words help you in catching the attention of the audience, they are the oxygen of oration. Our brain always welcomes and loves something new which is connected to old information stored in our minds. Let me elaborate:

In the year 2016, I was attending a seminar a how to write a book. During his talk, the speaker said, "To become an authorpreneur, all you need to do is sell 5,000 copies in India." Author, entrepreneur are common words but I never heard this word earlier "*authorpreneur.*" He instantly had my attention by that time. I got involved.

5. Speak like authority: I remember presenting as a public speaking conference as a host at MS Talks and the next speaker was Professor Kulvinder Singh and his topic was - How to live in the present?

So, I introduced his topic this way: "All of us know that we have to live in present, but we should always keep in mind that it has been '*pre-sent*' by God for us to live in present."

Professor Kulvinder as a keynote speaker noticed this bifurcation of *present to pre-sent* and began his speech like this,

"Sherry just gave a very nice explanation on the word present and I was not aware the breakup pre-sent. Please give a round of applause for Sherry first for giving me another perspective."

Through this *unrehearsed observation*, he connected brilliantly with everyone by showing humility and getting it acknowledged by the audience. So he impressed the host and audience both. He involved all of us.

*TED - Technology, Entertainment and Design

7 POWERFUL TECHNIQUES TO INCREASE THE AUDIENCE'S PARTICIPATION

As a public speaker, the biggest strength you can have is to be on top of your topic preparation, quality content and people engagement skills.

The biggest challenge for any public speaker is trepidation and connecting with the people in the room.

I have experienced that if your speech is audience-centered framing, you will most certainly get appraise by the audience to go a long way because they will never get bored.

Audience participation circumscribes a broad range of tools using various engaging activities which you can decide to give pleasure to the audience.

A speaker has to be proficient in his technique to introduce activity successfully.

HOW WILL YOU CHANGE THE ENERGY OF THE ROOM?

In one of my keynote on Leadership with Sirca Ltd. where I was addressing 100+ managers and dealers from pan India. After the introduction with the audience, I could sense that Sirca sales team people required a basic view of leadership to start with.

I simply used an easy-medium-difficult technique.

Remember, as munchkins, we were told to adapt – easy-medium -difficult technique in examinations. Firstly, attempt easy questions then medium followed by difficult.

Subtly, I kept on asking the questions out of answers given by the audience which can fit into their caliber to make it easy for the audience and generate interest.

Audience loves the fact that if the speaker has asked something, we have answered it. It gives them contagious pleasure. Secondly, if one person has answered and got applaud the second one feels I would love to be in the limelight too. That's all you need to connect.

"If your audience is not listening, it's not their fault.
It's yours."

—Seth Godin

Here I am sharing some powerful techniques for you to increase the audience participation:

1. I.E.I. Formula: In an interview, Chairman of Aakash Institute Mr. JC Chaudhry once said, "You cannot change certain things in the education system, they are irreplaceable. The policy and philosophy of talk and chalk are still not replaceable."

Likewise, there are three things that are irreplaceable in public speaking.

Inform: Ensure you have something worth to inform your audience.

Educate: Take responsibility to make sure your talk has key learnings for everyone to provide self-education.

Inspire: Despite the first two, your talk should inspire to take action.

Include **I.E.I.** formula when you are preparing the structure of your speech because it is still irreplaceable and one of the core techniques to engage the audience.

2. Let audience talk through activity: I have attended a Start-up business seminar at Taj Vivanta, Delhi where the speaker was talking about the topic; passion.

How an entrepreneur can follow passion facing challenges?

The biggest huddle for the speaker was to have people in the common mindset first in the hall about the booms and busts of a business.

He came up with an engagement activity of 10 minutes, before going to a lunch break.

In an audience hall of 150+, he divided people in the group of 8- 10 by asking them to move the face to the audience sitting in the back row. This way in no time, teams were created in the groups, and all you need to do was to share your passion and challenges with each of your group members.

We all love to talk and especially the ones who burned the bridge. They feel now is the opportunity. This technique of sharing their passion has made everyone interact, listen to each other who were strangers a few hours back.

Boy, it was a buzz all over!! The room's energy was at an all-time high level for the day.

What a high engagement technique I learnt that day. You can also use it for any specific engagement you wish to perform. It is effective and works successfully with a large audience.

So, let the *audience speak* in groups wherever you feel to include it in your talk. It is a powerful technique for audience participation.

3. Engage by framing the right question: I was listening to the public speaker in a seminar and he confessed openly that till some years back public speaking had him shiver in legs and his English was very weak until he learnt the art of public speaking and now have turned it around.

I am talking about Shantanu Gupta who is the communication advisor to Baba Ramdev (monk in India) and alumni ambassador of the Institute of Development Studies, University of Sussex, in India.

I got a chance to interact and listen to Mr. Shantanu Gupta - *TEDx speaker, author of the famous book 'The Monk who became Chief Minister' (a biography of Yogi Adityanath, the 21st Chief Minister of Uttar Pradesh) and political analyst.*

Shantanu came at the podium and just before his speech commenced, the audience was feeling thirsty and they all scattered except a few sitting in the front rows and others started checking their notifications on the mobile handset.

An awkward situation for a respectable figure but a common sight too;

Notice the technique now, how he engaged with the audience.

Seeing the stampede behind, Shantanu showed the nerve to walk his way and smartly shifted his gears and framed a right question to the front row audience.

Hey guys," What have been your expectations from this program?"

His framing was across – 'expectations.' The audience loves to talk about expectations, whether it can be wise or not.

And individually he came to everyone and gathered a few answers, by that time everyone was settled in the back.

In this scenario, it was all about reading and taking charge of the situation with the remaining audience and he was exceptional in his approach. This is where experience speaks.

Few minutes and his talk started…

As a speaker, *framing the right question* is crucial.

Framed question has to be as alluring as your recent experience of watching a latest Bollywood movie or buying a new mobile handset or any hot news.

Audience should not feel that they are in the spotlight and feel nervous about the question; rather they get a feeling of competence to engage.

Creating a competent environment for the audience has to be your number one priority and everything is secondary.

Another metaphor to learn the art of framing the right question from the audience:

Who all can tell what leadership is?

Can be replaced with

Who all are here to learn about leadership?

You will notice comparatively higher engagement by the audience in the second one.

The framing is *'learning'*. Everyone loves to learn.

Isn't it?

This takes me to the next technique.

4. Engage through music, dance: This technique is optional depending on the sensitivity of the event or the talk you are engaged in. But it is a popular technique, a lot of networking platforms and motivational speakers love to engage the audience using music along-with motivational speeches. As a speaker, the highest form of energy is created when the audience feels high. I was speaking on the same grounds to India's one of the sough-after motivational speaker, sales trainer Mr. TS Madaan to which he said,

In Hindi: *"Yaar Sherry, Main to sabse pehle jaate hi dhol aur music bajwa deta hu,aur sabko bolta hu chalo mil kar nachte hai*

aur life ko celeberate karte hai. Ekdum room ka mahaul hi alag ho jaata hai."

In English: *"Dear Sherry, I go and play the drum and music and tell everyone to dance and enjoy together and celebrate life. The environment of the room changes radically."*

Through dance and music, a speaker can have the highest level of engagement. Try this effective technique shared by one of my mentor Sh. T S Madaan who is one of the most sought after speaker, trainer from India.

5. Engage by calling a volunteer on the podium: I have attended many TEDx talks where a speaker invites a volunteer on the podium and it creates amazing engagement amongst the audience.

Again, be sure what kind of audience you cater and you have a *key message to convey* when you apply this technique.

One of my dear friend and TEDx speaker Pratik Uppal who has delivered this powerful talk on - "Why do we fear speaking on stage?" has used this powerful technique in his talk.

Watch this talk at 8:10 if you wish to see only the engagement part by the speaker.

Link: *https://www.youtube.com/watch?v=LgKDXeV7Umo*

6. Engagement by reading affirmations with the audience: Most of us have created mental blocks in our minds due to our past experiences of life. Affirmations are one of the powerful ways to remove your mental blocks.

I followed this affirmations technique with my audience as a host in MS Talks public speaking conference - May which not only enlightened everyone but also created a positive aura in the room with immense engagement that too in little over 2 minutes. In fact, one of the attendees felt so connected that he instantly thanked me for in front of the packed audience.

I was able to inspire that individual profoundly.

If you wish to see the affirmations I have used, check it out.

Affirmation notes link: *https://www.evernote.com/shard/ s415/nl/156716862/2905b46d-d93f-4a7b-9c05-b4962d9e 3080?title=%23affirmations%20%23ms%20talks%20%23notes*

7. Engagement through meditation: At various mindfulness seminars or workshops I have attended in the past; state of mind plays a major role when you want to learn something. Audience, most of the times, are in a different state of mind due to distractions around life's challenges.

To align everyone with the talk or to break the ice, many speakers utilize the simple meditation technique tool and the results are phenomenal.

Not only one feels relaxed but also speaker gains the honest attention of the audience and it turns out to be a very effective engagement technique.

If involving everyone was easy, everyone would have become a speaker.

I am sure by now that you have a few good ideas to implement them in your sessions as a public speaker and please do share your feedback.

CHAPTER TWELVE

HOW TO ROCK THE STAGE AS A SPEAKER?

"The worst speech you'll ever give, will be far better than the one you never give."

–Fred Miller

After delivering several talks and listening to various experts and speakers, I researched this relevant information which can benefit you as a public speaker or being an orator with regular speech delivery sessions.

1. Opener in the first 30 seconds: Jim Cathcart is a renowned public speaker from America. He delivered his TEDx talk in 2013 and that's how he started using a prop [*]acon - fruit of oak tree

"Somewhere deep inside, you know what kind of person you were designed to be.

---

* Acorn - an oval nut that grows on an oak tree and has an outer part shaped like a cup

If you want to produce great acorns, think like an oak, not like an acorn.

Think like the person you intend to become, like the Christian question: what would Jesus do?

Ask yourself, how would the person I'd like to do the things I am about to do."

(63 words; 30 seconds)

TEDx Talk link: *https://www.youtube.com/watch?v=-ki9-oaPwHs*

This is how I started my keynote at Lovely Professional University on August 19, 2018, in front of the crowd of 150 people.

"Today in this auditorium, all the people sitting over here have three things in common,

Your past, your present and your future.

Your past has given you the strength and wisdom to enjoy life today and excel in the future."

(40 words; 42 seconds)

All I am saying is a work well begun is half done. Learn the **'Stage Craft'**, it is my signature workshop on public speaking mastery for anyone willing to become a public speaker.

It creates a very strong connection amongst the audience with a key message and attention getting openning.

You have to develop and rehearse a well-crafted openning to gain the attention of your audience in the first 30 seconds especially if you are delivering a *keynote of 10-20 minutes.*

2. Yes response: I have attended an online session recently by T.Harv Eker. It was mind-boggling. He is phenomenal when it comes to creating value for people.

T.Harv Eker frequently takes acknowledgement from the audience in between his session like this – 'Yes or Yes'.

Even if you watch him during his talks, he uses this effective technique often to gain the attention of listeners. I had the same observation watching Lisa Nichols speeches using customarily - 'Yes -Yes!'

A message conveyed and then again 'Yes -Yes!'

That's how she takes confirmation of clarity from the audience.

In 2017 at the Trainer's camp, I attended a session of team building and after completion of each activity the facilitator Punkesh Chawla who is a Team performance coach was taking acknowledgment the same way from the audience - Yes or Yes! And everyone was smiling - There is no NO, so it is YES!

Punkesh gained reasonable attention from the audience with his energy levels too.

Why the best speakers in the industry do that? Don't they know what the meaning of NO is?

Well, there is a psychological reason behind it.

The more yes you have the more audience is connected to your message. The psychological patterns are more clear and outlets an open attitude for acceptance by the speaker. It is a very simple technique and yet how much neglected it is in today's time. The more yesses we gather, the more likely we are to succeed in capturing the attention of our ultimate proposal.

You can use any other powerful word like Indian motivational speaker Sandeep Maheshwari uses 'Asaan hai' meaning - It's easy and Vivek Bindra uses – 'Bounce Back'. It helps to the listeners to navigate in the affirmative direction.

3. Public speaking Ninja: [†]*Charles F Kettering was one of the inspiring speakers in USA. Asked if he wrote any part of his talks ever; he replied;*

---

†Charles F Kettering - Reference taken from the book - The quick and easy way to effective speaking - Dale Carnegie

"What I have to say is, I believe far too important to write down the paper. I prefer to write on my audience's mind, on their emotions, with every ounce of my being."

This is one way to realize your strength from within. Mind you – your inner strength has a major role to play in your talk. It gives you power. It creates a zone in the mind which only accepts winning for yourself and it is contagious for your listeners.

4. Elicit emotions: When a man is empowered with the influence of his feelings, his real self comes to the surface. The bars are down. The heat of his emotions has burned all barriers away. He acts spontaneously. He is natural.

People love to see someone well versed with the subject on the podium, at the same time they want to be only you. Meaning - Talking and sharing your own experiences and feelings and not tossing bookish knowledge.

To go for the glory, simply be you. After all, it's the performance of a lifetime.

5. Humor: Not necessarily you will get an opportunity for humor; it always depends on the kind of speaking assignment. However, it works wonders with speeches when you make it humorous by engaging your listeners.

Social scientists have demonstrated that an interactive audience is more easily persuaded than a passive one. I strongly recommend you to watch this humorous and inspiring talk - "we can fix it – Manoj Vasudevan."[‡]

[‡]*Manoj Vasudevan was also adjudged world champion of public speaking by Toastmasters International in 2017. I show this video to train my mentees on humor.*

CHAPTER THIRTEEN

POWER OF WORDS

"Feed the right words in your talk, that's your audience's fuel."
—Author Sherry

One fine day, while talking to a close friend; he used a word –

Sherry, it isn't a jigsaw puzzle, you will be through.

I stressed "Which puzzle? "with an inquisitive mind.

He remarked – Jigsaw puzzle!

Then, he explained to me the meaning of jigsaw as I don't use the word much in my conversations and it wasn't stored in my sub-conscious. This small conversation w gave me a clue about how important it is to switch the words which the audience can co-relate with easily to make your speech overwhelming.

If I ask you;

How do you understand the meaning of any discussion in a conversation with any recipient while talking?

Simple. You both use and understand common language, words and emotion to communicate and the conversation becomes mesmerizing or vice versa.

Effective speakers use this analogy as their preeminent tool. They chose simple words strategically to convey their message. Surprisingly enough, I listened to many speeches where I found keywords usage too which is up to 10% in total speech content.

HOW TO CALCULATE THE WORDS PER MINUTE OF YOUR TALK?

You can use words in the speech by knowing how to calculate the words per minute of your talk.

1. Write any script on the MS word file, on the left side bottom it shows the word count.

2. Read the script. Record your voice using voice recorder available on mobile with your original speech style (includes pauses, intonation and stress)

3. Take a count till where you covered as per MS word file and you will get words per minute as per your rate of speech.

MY WORDS PER MINUTE IS – 90 – 100 WORDS PER MINUTE

Following the same method of words per minute, you can create your script with the exact number of minutes which is very useful in talks like TED, community talks, keynotes at conferences where they expect you to speak or cover the topic in 10 or 15 minutes. Every minute and second counts there.

Assuming 100 words per minute multiply 15 minutes =1500 words

If your talk is on success, add 10% "success" as your keyword.

150 times use the word "success". It has a psychological effect.

To paint a word picture of any experience, a smart speaker prefers using the full range of multisensory phraseology which will etch the event upon the consciousness of the listeners.

The speakers disseminate attention. Yes, they do. Yes, I do it too. Yes, the expert does it too. I know, what you are saying, Yes I do it as well.

By the way; we used YES four times in a row. Crazy! (:

After all your purpose is to make your audience see what you saw, hear what you heard, and feel what you felt. The only way you can possibly achieve this effect is to use an abundance of concrete details.

I try to include many points and the right words to impress my audience through preparation in the right direction. That's always there.

One day my friend called me as he was feeling disheartened.

He spoke in a dispirited tone, "I did a stupid mistake."

I asked, "What happened?"

He said, "As you know I own a diesel fuel engine car, the fuel station attendant filled petrol in the car as I was on phone and wasn't attentive.

I had to get all the petrol out from the tank and after 3-4 hours of work it finally happened and I got the diesel."

I laughed harder than I should have.

I asked him, "So what was the learning?" He said, "I can't move a diesel car by filling petrol inside.

For that, I need diesel only. That's what drives my car. I have to feed the right fuel.

Diesel is my car's fuel and not petrol."

I learned that day that I have to feed my audience mind reservoir with chosen words connected to my topic.

That's what drives my audience. I have to feed the right words.

That's my audience's fuel.

CHAPTER FOURTEEN

SPONTANEITY: ART OF PUBLIC SPEAKING

"Grasp the subject, the words will follow."

—Cato The Elder

There is much more you need to experience and register in your mind when it comes to public speaking on a podium.

Practice the talk, visualizing the talk, catchy content and most important - 'Delivery of your speech' is what makes it cogent and you end up getting applaud as a great rhetorician by writing your content in the minds of your audience.

Even if you are well prepared, spontaneity is what saves you due to any adversity thrown at you by nature or ineptitude.

Hey! I also learned an important aspect of public speaking that day and it was - spontaneity.

2 years back at TEDxCVS an event organized by College of Vocational Studies (CVS), New Delhi India. I witnessed an amazing preparation by the college students and the TEDx organizing team of CVS. They were highly exuberant as it was

their first-ever event of college after the license approval by TED.*

When the turn of first speaker Sam *(name changed)* came to deliver his speech, the mic stopped working which inevitably break the flow of the speaker.

After a few seconds, Sam re-started his speech.

Guess what?

In another minute, the wireless presenter used for presentation stopped working. Sam was pressing the button but nothing happened, he smiled and again the talk was stopped.

Audience - Thinking what's going on here. (:

Being a speaker and a trainer, I read the situation and immediately rush towards car parking as I was carrying my training kit alongside the laptop bag in the car. I fetch my presenter and gave it to one of their organizing committee member.

Anyways, it wasn't applied for use as it was already arranged by the organizing team when I came back. The guy heartily thanked me for rushing and bringing it to avoid a flop and kept it till the end of the event with him.

What must be going on in the speaker's mind by this time?

The situation was orthodox, irritating and worst as nothing was going in favor of Sam and it was conspicuous to the audience.

Sam quickly realized the essence of the audience losing interest in him. To bring the smile on audience faces, he breaks the ice laughed and said,

"Hey!! No more interruptions hopefully now - addressing the audio visual team. Please restart the video recording, I will do it from the beginning."

---

*TED - Technology, Entertainment and Design

"The capacity to learn is a gift; the ability to learn is a skill; the willingness to learn is a choice - Brian Herbert

I learnt about - Spontaneity! Spontaneity beats nervousness.

Sam being an experienced orator quickly adapted the weak areas because in the end it was his performance that mattered for everyone in the auditorium.

I also suggest you to read the book 'Lose to win' by the ace author Mr. Mukesh Bhatnagar which covers rich experiences of speakers and their real stories shared on MS Talks.

It was all set and talks were about to be given by six speakers on their real-life stories. That day, I attempted to memorize the script of my opening talk and decided to use 'apple' as a prop in the metaphor.

The event started on time and we all were very excited because this time MS Talks event was happening on a bigger scale compared to previous events.

It's 3.57 pm Sherry! I told myself and instructed the cameraman for coverage of the podium and my talk well.

As I began the event, I said the opening statement and that very moment I forgot the next few lines of the metaphor in the script. Butterflies started gushing in my stomach. What to do? I was highly strung at that time but kept smiling.

At that very moment, I completely forgot that I am a professional speaker and a corporate trainer who has delivered numerous talks already.

Duff! I need a glass of water. I drink the water; it was all getting recorded.

Behaving extempore, I took the charge using my presence of mind and opting to be myself in the situation rather than being 100% scripted. Being yourself and acting spontaneously in that situation proved out to be *a comeback*.

I decided to take the aerial route and spoke to the audience of around 50 people present that time this way- *"It happens in public speaking...Right!"*, *trying to find some smiling faces who can truly understand what I just went through.*

I covered up sensibly and using spontaneity convey a brave message to my sub conscious mind," *I wouldn't give up; I am here to inspire. It is my part, I own it."*

I will never forget that small interaction going on inside my brain while gulping glass of cold water. It was all happening in the fraction of a few seconds. That interaction with myself was the original me telling myself to stay focused.

Happens! Gear up. This is exactly what you need to coach people and how awesome it is experiencing the same yourself. Preach it Lion! Cheers. This simple statement changed my mind.

My deep understanding of physiology and oratory experience helped me get the confidence back in no time. After the event, I told myself seeing the podium - Getting there is easy, remaining yourself there takes guts. It does Sherry.

Tips for spontaneity in public speaking

1. You are performing for your audience first and not for you. Focus on your message and not on anything else.

2. Develop your mind with quick-witted thoughts by regularly reading books, blogs you adore which will back you up when you are in no man's land in certain situations.

3. The primary focus should always be the audience who is there to get learning from you being a role model.

4. Recover quick. Audience wants you to perform, entertain and inspire.

5. Keep your check points clear in your mind.

WHY TEDX TALK IS POPULAR IN PUBLIC SPEAKING?

"Brevity is a great charm of eloquence."

—Cicero

Many speakers assume TEDx is like just another talk given at any platform but it isn't.

My experience is you need to be very specific with your vocabulary, storytelling, orchestrating your rehearsals and more importantly bringing curiosity and excitement to make it memorable for the live audience as well as the YouTube audience who will watch it post upload.

TED is a non-profit organization founded by Richard Saul Wurman & Harry Marks.

It became more popular post 2009 when the talks delivered were uploaded on YouTube and it got viral and TEDx is an extension of TED platform.

TEDx is license based issued by TED in association with different educations and worthy individuals.

Effective communication is about brevity and that's how most of the TEDx talks are delivered. I am a 3 times TEDx speaker till January 2020. My experience says, it requires a different level of preparation.

You got to have that special element to deliver a TEDx talk because you are supposed to share an idea unheard before.

I have read this incident in one of the books from Brian Tracy;

There was once a meeting planner who phoned a professional speaker to book him for an upcoming event. The planner's first question was

"How much do you charge?"

The speaker replied, "It depends on the length of the talk you want me to give and the amount of time it takes for preparation."

The meeting planner then asked, "How much would you charge for a thirty-minute talk, and how long would it take to prepare?"

The speaker replied, "For a thirty-minute talk, it would require six to eight hours to prepare, and the fee would be $5,000."

The meeting planner was surprised. "How much would you charge for a half-day talk, and how long would it take to prepare?" he asked.

The speaker replied, "For a half-day talk, it would take about three to four hours to prepare, and it would cost $4,000."

"What about a full-day talk? How much is that?"

"That would only cost $3,000."

"How long would you require to prepare?" asked the meeting planner.

"Oh," said the speaker, "if it is a full-day talk, I can start now."

The Shorter the Talk, the More Difficult

The less you speak, the more you need to prepare. It requires precision and solid delivery with excellent non-verbal cues.

SUBMISSION

What is your little voice in the brain saying?

Was it worth it reading the book?

What has been your major takeaway from the book?

I've said this earlier, and I'll say it again as many times as you want:

"Talk is cheap, Action is everything."

I hope you enjoyed reading this book, but more importantly, I hope you use the techniques to improve and enhance the quality of speaking you do.

In my experience, reading alone will not make the difference you are looking for.

Reading is a start, but if you want to succeed in the real world, it's going to be your actions that count.

Beware of the little voice in your head saying something like:

"Rehearsals, Time waste... I will be speaking
my impromptu on stage...

I don't need or have time for rehearsals." Notice who is doing the talking here? The conditioned mind, that's who! Remember, it's job is to keep you right where you are, in your comfort zone. Don't listen to it. Do the action exercises, do your rehearsals, practice to the epitome and watch yourself emerging better than other speakers all the time.

I know mostly speakers are overconfident about their caliber but if you stick to your basics right and do what I said to you in this book, I promise you will thank me for all the advice.

You will be speaking like a king and impressing your audience giving for a standing ovation!

I also suggest you reread this book from beginning to end at least once a month for the next year. "What?" your little voice might be screaming. "I've already read the book, why do I need to read it over and over again?" Great question and the answer is simple: repetition is the mother of all skills and a sweet cousin of mastery.

Again, the more you study this book, the faster the concepts will become natural and automatic for you.

Professional Speaking is the next big industry in India and you will see this statement becoming a reality.

I will work in this field till my last breath to promote presentation literacy in India.

That is my contribution to the nation and skill development for the nation.

I am a down to earth guy and I wish people start saying,

This guy we met from India is a great communicator or an excellent public speaker creator.

90% of the work profiles in India require strategic communication, presentations and almost all the leadership profiles require public speaking to promote your thoughts, persuade people and gain in monetary terms in the business.

Communication and Public Speaking is the best thing ever happened in my life and I enjoy my success.

As I stated earlier, I learned my way of public speaking success, so now it's my turn to assist others to become efficient speakers and still learning from achievers and orators around.

There is never a last leg of learning, there is so much to learn and I love to live like a learner and not as an expert because this feeling helps me to keep my mindset open and learn from my trainees too many a times.

In reality, we all learn from each other.

My mission is to "educate and inspire people and create '1 million speakers in India by the year-end 2030.'

I remember while I was doubting myself to say this publicly on a Facebook live, my faith only encouraged me – Go ahead Sherry, success belongs to those who are humble and think big.

Stay humble and Think Big.

I help people based on their passion, zeal, purpose, and joy versus fear, need, and obligation."

I am truly blessed to have seminars, workshops, and meetups that transform people's lives quickly and permanently. I'm thrilled to have been able to help over 1,00,000 people through my trainings and events I organize and inspire the social media community of over 1,70,000 people at MS Talks.

We organize MS Talks every month, you can learn from different styles of speeches and delivery by various speakers from the fraternity. I feel proud of myself that we are consistently doing MS Talks events and making a real difference in the lives of the people around.

As I quote, it is 'Inspiration from anywhere' and you will find your way.

From my heart to yours, I invite you to attend my Public Speaking Mastery Workshop.

This event will take you to an entirely new level of success and transformation in public speaking.

Post workshop, if required, I do one on coaching and that is where I actually change your speaking style and help right on the spot to make sure you become a great public speaker.

Feel free to enquire for my one on one coaching programs on public speaking.

It doesn't matter which part of the world you are from. Don't worry I am teaching mentees online through my webinars as well with equal success. I give them exercises and assignments and make them feel like physical training.

Well, that's it for now. Thank you for spending your precious time reading this book. I wish you tremendous success and true happiness, and I look forward to meeting you in person soon.

For your success,

Author Sherry